WHEN WOLVES COME

Navana Winston

WHEN WOLVES COME

Please contact: Navana Winston

Email: Globalharvest4U@gmail.com

Cover Design: Red 31 Advertising and Design Bureau

Publisher: www.brandgrowth.co.za
Preston Jongbloed, Brandgrowth.
preston@brandgrowth.co.za

ISBN: 978-0-620-98951-0

To my 7 children who have shared me with the world.
In my darkest moments, you kids became my reason for fighting to
stay alive, so young, so tender
and I was so sorry for the pain I had caused.
Loving you forever Mom

CONTENTS

FOREWORD

It was over 15 years ago, when I first met Navana in Georgia through a mutual brother in Christ. Later that day, at dinner the Lord began to reveal to my husband and I "in part" various details concerning the current phase and future of her journey in Christ. After dinner, we had no idea that over the course of many months the Holy Spirit would begin the process of knitting our hearts together.

When I look back and survey "her process" and all the Lord has done in Navana throughout the years we've known each other, I can truly say, "This is the Lord's doing; it is marvelous in our eyes." Psalms 118:23 KJV. It is marvelous in my eyes to have had the privilege to observe her love, faith, commitment to Christ and personal resolve to stay on course, serve and please the Lord. Because of her love for Christ, the gospel and people she has consistently chosen and learned to choose through what she has suffered to take the narrow road when faced with rejection, heartache, disappointment, fear, misunderstanding and a host of other spiritual and people challenges or their memories.

And now that another phase of her journey is complete, my heart is filled with joy, anticipation and great expectation for all of the fruit that will continually come forth because she continues to say yes to the Lord. I am also excited for you the reader because you can now glean from various parts of her life's journey and be healed, made aware and equipped.

What you're about to read is no joke or made-up story. So, if you're ready to be healed, equipped or made aware. Let this part of "your process" begin.

Apostle Ida Thornton-PTMI
Smyrna, GA

As I was reading the stories at the beginning of this book concerning wolves, it dawned on me that many believers and ministers alike are susceptible to the destructive force of wolves because they lack a key component of the Apostle's mantle – A Father's covering. Within the mantle of a true apostle is the heart of a father towards their spiritual sons and daughters.

I Corinthians 4:15 states, for though you might have ten thousand instructors in Christ, yet you do not have many fathers; for in Christ Jesus I have begotten you through the gospel.

Apostle Paul Thornton-PTMI
Smyrna, GA

Life is comprised of many wonderful things. It is in itself an amazing journey. As we travel throughout our own lifetime, our experiences will take us to a variety of different places. Some overflowing with joy, while other places are filled with sorrow and pain. We can go to the valley of the shadow of death or up the mountain of contentment. We can travel to down and out boulevard or make our home in the dumps. Others never get past a place called nowhere. Day in and day out, like weary travelers we trod through life often without realizing God has a resting-place for the heavy- laden sin sick soul. If you find yourself or someone you care about on a cliff, at the point of no return, tell them there is a path that leads to restoration where the healing waters flow.

Enclosed you will find the directional insights to a place called whole as I share with you a tale of a betrayal woven in a web of deception. A well thought out plan devised by an enemy who has come to devour and destroy your soul. I made this journey to a place called whole and greater is He who lives in me, he is greater than he who abides in this world, for today I'm safe and living in this place.

The kingdom of God is no place for fairy tales and childhood games, yet they are played out in the church every day. Better known as lies and deceit, the foolishness of man's heart will open him to the wiles of the enemy and destroys the unwatchful soul. These are the devices of the enemy. Proceed with caution and let the church beware - the sheep have encountered the wolf on the road.

"And I say, lest any man beguile you with enticing words."
Colossians 2:4 KJV

CHAPTER ONE

THE BOY WHO CRIED WOLF

There was a little boy who cried wolf. Everyone would run to the town square to assist him, but there would be no wolf. Every day he would do this and every day the town's people would come in vain. One day the real wolf came and the little boy cried and cried and cried, but nobody came to his rescue and the wolf devoured him whole.

Just a fictional childhood story sometimes told at bedtime, the moral was to teach us, don't cry wolf if there isn't one. Parents have used it to teach children the value of honesty and the danger of telling lies. But what about the real wolves, the ones that dare come to the church, or the ones we encounter on life's road The ones attempting to devour us, what do we do when they come? How do we know who they are? how do we, the sheep, the Lords children deal with modern day wolves? Who is going to hear our cry? How can we protect ourselves or even hope to recover from his deadly wound?

First, we must identify when personal insecurities and fears create skepticism and paranoia. This potent mix of anxiety and anticipation usually surrounds our own activities and thoughts of failure leaving us looking and expecting to be victimized.

Some Christians have made it a personal point to live as professional victims. Always-giving life to unfounded fears and un-impending dangers. It is dangerous for the believer to constantly harbor and confess fear. We call those things that are not, as though they were and before we know it the thing that lived with you only as a fear has now become an ever-present reality.

Job recorded it this way, "For the thing which I greatly feared is come upon me, and that which I was afraid of is come unto me."- Job 3:25 KJV

We must watch and be aware of our fears, for the things we fear often reveal the insecurities we have. Insecurity about who we are and what we have. Many of us even harbor insecurities about the blessings of God. We don't feel deserving of these blessings, so we are always apprehensive about losing them. There are others who fear success more than they fear the thought of their own failure so they are constantly crying doom and despair. They live in a realm where failure becomes a cycle of life. It provides a valid way of escape from the responsibility of true success in Christ Jesus.

Like the little boy whose imaginary wolf becomes a reality, no one will jump to come to your rescue because of your reputation of harboring and perpetuating your fears. We need to choose to be set free and true deliverance is not in a prayer line where the evil is constantly being cast away from our presence and out of our lives. True and lasting freedom occurs when we embrace the infallible word of God and allow it to pierce through the strongholds of our thoughts. This is the process of renewing our minds and it happens when the word enters into our hearts transforming the mind with truth and light. Let the power of His word pierce and shatter your fear, it will also dry up your tears.

"For God hath not given us the spirit of fear; but of power, and of love, and of a sound mind." - II Timothy 1:7 KJV

What a powerful statement of truth, that the inheritance of the saints doesn't include the bondage of fear. Our legacy from God is one of power, love and soundness of mind. I will not deny that fear is a real element in life, but I will say that it must be turned to its most fruitful state where it has the power to produce the fruits of righteousness.

"The fear of the Lord is the beginning of knowledge: but fools despise wisdom and instruction". - Proverbs 1:7 KJV

So that thou incline thine ear unto wisdom and apply thine heart to understanding. Then shalt thou understand the fear of the Lord and find the knowledge of God." - Proverbs 2:2, 5 KJV

"Be not wise in thine own eyes: fear the Lord, and depart from evil."
Proverbs 3:7 KJV

It is an evil thing to constantly walk in unmerited fears, this opens the door to destruction and the wolf will surely come.

Chapter Overview

One can only imagine this young man's desperate need for attention at any and all cost. He would risk mass hysteria and divert resources from other more important needs just for a false alarm. Often it is a person of intense loneliness and/or inner insecurity that will go to such lengths to be the center of such toxic attention.

How often has someone been guilty of tying the hands and time of others, or even making friends with unwarranted issues of little or no importance just for attention? Other times there can be a real mental or medical issue behind such behavior such as PTSD, which can be caused by trauma, this can lead to intense paranoia and suspicion at the smallest incident. Mental health is a real issue that should not be avoided or stigmatized.

In every situation take time in prayer to seek the counsel of God and get to the real root of such issues, don't be so quick to blame everything on the Devil. Busy he is, but he is not everywhere all the time.

CHAPTER TWO

LITTLE RED RIDING HOOD

Little Red Riding Hood was on her way to visit her sick grandmother with gifts of love and cheer when she crossed paths with a wolf and made the mistake of telling the wolf what she was up to. Being the wicked creature that he is; he ran ahead of her, tied up grandma, locked her in the closet and took her place on the bed of affliction and infirmity to await little Reds arrival. Little Red does not immediately discover his deception, but gradually begins to question his appearance. Knowing he is about to be exposed, he leaps from the bed and pounces on Little Red. Unlike the little boy in the last story, a good woodsman hears her cry, comes to her rescue, drives off the wolf, and releases grandma from her uncomfortable captivity.

Like Little Red many of us make the same mistake. When we encounter the wolf on the road to destiny, we tell him all we know about the plans of God for our lives, where we are going and whom we will be meeting without ever realizing the nature of the character we are talking to. The wolf takes what we've given him and runs ahead up the road posing as the real thing, while disrupting the will of God in our lives. Precious time is lost, unable to be recovered and many suffer the hardship of captivity while waiting for our eyes to be opened to the truth that we have been deceived.

Many young women are just like Little Red covered in the blood on the outside, but not in the heart and the wolf meets us on the road of life. Whether he is tall, dark and handsome, blonde and blue-eyed, riding in a Lincoln or a Limousine, it is the lust in our own heart that blinds us and draws us away. The wolf was not as interested in Little Red as he was in what she was carrying. Like her, we allow wolves to peak into the goody bags of our spiritual womb. They see the anointing, the vision, and the purposes of God. They see the gifts of the Spirit and the call that will open doors. They see that our womb is pregnant with rich revelation waiting to be birthed. Don't be deceived. He does not want what you are, he doesn't even want you, instead he wants what you have, the treasure you are carrying.

Like Little Red, you will later encounter this wolf in some form of affliction waiting to lure you with his appearance in your hour of weakness. He will appeal to your deep sense of compassion to come closer, to feed him out of the wealth of your inheritance. Moments before the risk of exposure, when he sees your heart questioning the validity of his appearance, he will pounce on you with all fours to capture and hold you down and to paralyze you with the fear of his presence. He smothers you with the heat of his words. He has you just where he wants you, cut off from everyone who cares and cut off from any sign of hope or help. There you are hopeless and discouraged waiting for the moment when your torment will end.

Hold on, receive this into your spirit if you are in the clutches of a wolf, don't be so quick to give up the ghost. Like the good woodsman, the Father of Glory is waiting to hear your cry. Holler loud and holler now, Help! Wolf in the House!

The psalmist said it like this, "I cried unto the Lord with my voice, and he heard me out of his holy hill. Selah" - Psalms 3:4 KJV

"The Lord hear thee in the day of trouble; the name of the God of Jacob defend thee; send help thee help from the sanctuary, and strengthen thee out of Zion." - Psalms 20:1-2 KJV

"I will cry unto God most high; unto God that performeth all things for me. He shall send from heaven, and save me from the reproach of him that would swallow me up. Selah. God shall send forth his mercy and his truth." - Psalms 57:2-3 KJV

"Now know I that the Lord saveth his anointed; he will hear him from his holy heaven with the saving strength of his right hand." - Psalms 20:6 KJV

Isn't it wonderful to know that no matter what our distress God will hear us when we cry and call unto him? He will deliver you. Aside from the fact that God can save you, you must choose to go continually to the wisdom and knowledge of God's word to remain in a safe place. You must glean from your captivity by realizing what ensnared you. Ask yourself, how did the wolf lure me into stopping to talk to him?

The story speaks profoundly to women and men, but especially to women in ministry. Pastors, evangelists, prophets. apostles and teachers; we must not entertain the fear of not being capable of performing the task God has given us. As women, we continue to cultivate the thought that God only called us because he could not find a man. Where does that leave us when a capable man does come along? We often sell ourselves short and like Little Red, instead of hurrying on to accomplish the task we were given we stop to explain what we are doing. We lack the wisdom needed to know that when God is using you to move through realms of darkness to deliver healing, comfort, encouragement and virtue to another wounded vessel you don't stop along the way to entertain strangers. This displayed that her heart still held an amount of undetected foolishness.

"Even a fool, when he holdeth his peace, is counted wise: and he that shutteth his lips is esteemed a man of understanding." - Proverbs 17:28 KJV

"A fool's mouth is his destruction, and his lips are the snare of his soul." - Proverbs 18:7 KJV

Red was traveling through the forest and everyone knows that the forest is darker than the open plain. It holds hidden dangers and creatures of prey. Her own personal pride causes her to stop and her foolishness led her to talk.

*"Pride goeth before destruction and a haughty spirit before a fall" -
Proverbs 16:18 KJV*

Here is Little Red in her bright new coat carrying the food that
will feed the sickened soul. She was entrusted with a great task
on a dangerous journey through the forest alone. A wise woman
would have avoided the wolf altogether. She certainly wouldn't
have stopped to talk to him. A humble woman would not have seen
herself as a potential match for this untimely appearance of a total
stranger. She would not have stopped to boast of her possessions
and accomplishments.

Red boasted about her new garments. She boasted about her ability
to carry precious cargo. She boasted about her fearless, but foolish
journey in the forest. Alone. Never go alone. She foolishly reveals
her possessions; and allowed a wolf to peek into her basket. No
church or leader should uncover the secrets of their vision to a
stranger. Many who have entertained strangers have entertained
angels unaware, this includes fallen angels of darkness. No church
should do this, but women who are in pastoral ministry are at a
considerably higher risk because the real wolves tend to seek them
out first.

Particularly women who lack the parental counsel and supervision
of governmental oversight, no apostle, no bishop, no outside and
little in-house prophetic counsel. This state of solitude attracts
wolves and they see you as open prey. You lend credibility to their
suspicions by stopping and revealing what God has concealed in
your care. You expose the plan of God without any idea about the
nature of the spirit you are entertaining. Who is he? Where did he
come from? What does he want with me? Don't think it's your
good looks or slick hairdo or your clean sleek physical condition or
vivacious curves. It is the Anointing that he is after. The presence
of the spirit of God is what he wants to rape you of. He wants to
strip you of that light which shines out of your intimacy with God
and when your countenance is darkened, He will leave you there.

Some instruction comes beforehand and some instruction comes in
hindsight. Beforehand God speaks these words,

"Do you think that the scripture saith in vain, the spirit that dwelleth in us lusted to envy? But he giveth more grace. Wherefore he saith, God resisted the proud, but giveth grace unto the humble. Submit yourselves therefore to God. Resist the devil, and he will flee from you. Draw nigh unto God, and he will draw nigh to you. Cleanse your hands, he sinners; and purify your hearts, ye double minded. Be afflicted, and mourn, and weep; let your laughter be turned to mourning, and your joy to heaviness. Humble yourselves in the sight of the Lord, and he shall lift you up."-James 4:5-10 KJV

If in the times of darkness and danger we would draw unto the presence of God, we would find safety and counsel, but we don't do that. Just like Little Red, many of us stopped to flirt with the wolf. We saw his alligator shoes, the sparkling glitter of gold on his hand, his glistening smile and the aroma of his cologne mingled with the scent of his masculinity. Never mind he's wearing a suit that lays on him as perfect as the grass lays on the meadow, and right there while you're still beholding what appears to be his glory something happens.

The writer James explains it like this: "Let no man say when he is tempted, I am tempted of God: for God cannot be tempted with evil, neither tempted he any man: But every man is tempted, when he is drawn away of his own lust, and enticed. Then when lust hath conceived, it bringeth forth sin: and sin, when it is finished, bringeth forth death." - James 1:13-15 KJV

Sin is conceived in our hearts when we yield our wills to our carnal desires. When you lust after your desires, it becomes easy to compromise the word of God to satisfy them. Many times, we see the things around us that come to make us stumble and fall, but it takes the Holy Ghost of God to help us see the things within us. Even the Holy Ghost by Himself is not enough if we are not willing to work with Him in obedience. We may hear Him, but choose to resist and rebel against his gentle prompts. We must be willing to look and examine our own heart and motives in the light of God's word. Your enemy will never gain entrance without an open door somewhere; he desires to lure you into his bed. That old bed of iniquity where he seduces you with your own desires. The enemy we confront outwardly is not as dangerous as the enemy that lies within us. It is usually this inner enemy that we are very ignorant of. As a result, Satan thrives off of our refusal to look at the things that hide within us. If he sees that he cannot draw you to his bed he will be satisfied to simply devour you, destroy you, and leave you for dead.

"The thief cometh not, but for to steal, and to kill, and to destroy:" - *John 10:10 KJV*

Well, I suppose from time to time we've all had a Little Red in us. The danger is when we are not aware of it. Real victory and deliverance can take place when the eyes of our understanding are opened and we look through the eyes of the spirit to examine our own hearts and motives. You may not think this applies to you but be prayerful there's still a wolf on the loose.

Chapter Overview

How often have you been tempted to go off on your own to do what might have seemed like some menial task, only to find yourself in over your head or confronted with some unsuspecting danger? We can all move too quickly or just independently, most times out of impatience or even arrogance, even when we know we should wait or seek outside assistance. One of the other things that can compound this is our flirtatious nature with danger, some of us simply thrive off the risk involved with dangerous adventure.

How often have you heard of someone dying on a mountain trail while hiking alone or falling off of a cliff trying to take a picture of themselves alone? All of the examples of what can happen when we venture off into dark, dangerous, uncharted territory alone still is not enough to stop most of us from doing it at some point in our own lives so we will continue to hear of people's demise in such situations. Let's make a conscious effort not to go anywhere without the leading of the Holy Spirit, the counsel of our heavenly Father or the accompaniment of his mighty angels. Oh yes, and how about the release of your own human leadership/shepherd. Then if at all possible, you should take someone with you. We are all called to do some Kingdom work, but let us be safe out there.

Remember, regardless of what or who you've lost your greatest growth will come from finding yourself.

CHAPTER THREE

THE THREE LITTLE PIGS

Once upon a time, there were three little pigs, each decided it was time to leave home and establish something to call their own. The first pig went out, not really wanting to work hard at all, still needing a lot of time for play. He built his house of straw. The second went out a little more educated, but not really dedicated so he built his house better than his brother, he at least used wood. The third little pig, a laborer for sure, rolled up his sleeves and got to work. Brick by brick he started to build, line upon line as the industrious sort, and precept upon precept. He then gave his report. I've built a good house on rock and not sand; on a sure foundation. It is built to withstand every attack and trial close at hand. Brick by brick my structure went up. I worked and worked not stopping to play. I finished my job while it was day. They then all settled down to sleep in their houses that night. Two tired from play and the other from working all day.

The wolf is a creature that doesn't move in the light. He'd rather lay and wait for the night. Now at twilight's peak, he comes creeping up along the hedges, that old dirty sneak. Up to the houses he crept, the pigs unaware that an ever-increasing danger was there. To each little pig, he said the same, "Open the door right now, let me in; or I'll huff and I'll puff and blow your house in". Down came the straw and down came the wood, but the house made of brick was standing good. You know the rest of this story. The two lazy pigs escaped by a hair, but that third little pig the wolf did not scare. His words did not stir even a hair on his chin. The wolf ran for the chimney, in his anger he brewed. He had been better off to leave that last pig alone because when he came down from the chimney his butt was brewed. Well that's another cute story, but the moral is true, let's see what the word says about the little pig in you.

"Except the Lord build the house, they labour in vain that build it: except the Lord keep the city, the watchman waketh but in vain." - Psalms 127:1 KJV

We must be careful that whatever we put forth our hands to build is being erected to the glory of God. It must be what God has commanded you to do. Your motive for doing what he commands must be to benefit and advance the kingdom of God, never for your own personal gain. This is a crucial factor in the growth process of ministry. We must desire to truly know why we do the things we do. Is it for God and his glory or is some (or all) of it for me? Preachers must be very careful when they plan meetings and revivals for the sake of meeting budgets, generating finances and taking care of themselves. God does not obligate himself to monuments for man neither is he committed to fulfilling our selfish desires. Your desire must be to feed and nurture the flock of God. When your heart is set on fulfilling the will of God, the presence of God is always there to protect and provide for the things He has ordained. Again, beware! God is in no way obligated to fulfill or protect your personal ambitions, especially when your motive is self-centered.

Many ministries are being erected but they are not remaining. Because they are not equipped to withstand the onslaught of demonic attacks. You must have more than a desire to do a work for God. You must have a divine mandate from the Father himself. The Holy Spirit is committed to provide divine protection and provision to every vision being carried out according to the will of God. We must remember that good intentions are not always God's intentions.

Paul says it like this, "For we are labourers together with God: ye are God's husbandry, ye are God's building. According to the grace of God which is given unto me, as a wise master builder, I have laid the foundation, and another buildeth thereon. But let every man take heed how he buildeth thereupon. For other foundation can no man lay than that is laid, which is Jesus Christ. Now if any man builds upon this foundation gold, silver, precious stones, wood, hay, stubble; every man's work shall be made manifest: for the day shall declare it, because it shall be revealed by fire; and the fire shall try every man's work of what sort it is. If any man's work abide which he hath built thereupon, he shall receive a reward. If any man's work shall be burned, he shall suffer loss: but he himself shall be saved; yet so as by fire." - 1 Corinthians 3:9-15 KJV

We must be committed as Christians to build only on the foundation that God has laid. Our foundation is the Lord Jesus Christ and his doctrine.

Even in teaching us to pray the Lord directed us to pray, "Thy kingdom come, Thy will be done..." (Matthew 6:10 KJV)

Everything we do should be motivated by the word of God to establish the kingdom of God in the earth, in our lives, and in our hearts. Ask yourself these important questions – Don't be afraid to be honest before your heavenly Father.

- Am I working to be seen?
- Am I working to build a great name or a multi-million-dollar complex?
- Is my goal to obtain a powerful radio or television ministry?
- Exactly what is my underlying motive for doing the things I do?
- Are my motives kingdom-minded or carnal-minded?
- Am I building for me or for God?
- And, if I am building for God's kingdom, am I doing it wholeheartedly?

We must take careful consideration to the attitude with which we work for God. Whatever kingdom area we are building will affect more lives than just our own. Will God see you like the first lazy pig who only wanted to play and have a good time? He foolishly threw together a house of straw in order to waste away the rest of his time with worthless tasks and foolish play or perhaps he was idle with his time sleeping away the day.

"For when they shall say, Peace and safety; then sudden destruction cometh upon them; as travail upon a woman with child; and they shall not escape. But ye, brethren, are not in darkness, that that

day should overtake you as a thief. Ye are all the children of light, and the children of the day: we are not of the night, nor of darkness. Therefore let us not sleep, as do others; but let us watch and be sober."
- 1 Thessalonians 5:3-6 KJV

We have a responsibility as members of the household of faith to be balanced and sound in mind, not slumbering in the affairs of the kingdom. One of the reasons Satan has perpetrated so much evil against the children of God is because of our slothful inattentive attitudes. We are sleeping the greatest days of opportunity away. Many churches and believers are still lazily praying, waiting for a move of God and the spirit of God is already sweeping across the land. There is fresh oil pouring out on the remnants and there are many now drinking new wine. This move is not in the traditional church structure of man-made rules, regulations and bondages.The oil is not being poured heavily in churches where there is a clear and distinguished line drawn between the pulpit and pews, where the pastor's role instead of Christ is the major focal point.

Churches where there is not a corporate cooperative effort can find themselves lagging behind as the spirit sweeps thru yielded unrestricted ministries where no one is overly concerned about religious formalities, these are the ones who have laid aside every superficial, super spiritual weight and are crying out to God for a fresh touch. These churches have gotten the revelation that true end-time revival is being birth in prayer, love and unity. There is a prayer revival sweeping across the land in unprecedented proportions. People are consecrating their mouths in prayer. They have taken up their ranks in spiritual warfare and stomped out the murmuring, backbiting and devouring tongues from amongst themselves. Love is the new weapon of choice.

There must be a disciplined determination to serve God wholeheartedly. Where the heart is hungering for the more of God, the people are laying aside the weights of tradition, jealousy, envy and strife. They are emptying themselves. Allowing the old man to be poured out at the altar in repented prayer, weeping before the Lord, waiting for a fresh outpouring of the oil and the wine. Like the third industrious little pig, we must work while it is day. The first work must be done in us. If we have not prepared and strengthened ourselves with his presence, we will not have strength for the harvest. We will be like the lazy virgins who ran out of oil before the real journey ever started.

Prophetic warfare is effective when we enter into a realm of prayer that produces inner breaking, causing our souls to come into agreement with the word of God. It is here in his presence, under his anointing that we both speak and live his word, as it is written and revealed in unity with his spirit. It takes time to enter into this realm, which is one of the reasons it brings forth a revival of prayer. A purging takes place as the believer proceeds to press his or her way into this powerful place of prayer. It is a place where idle chatters cease and your tongue becomes a mighty weapon of war decreeing and declaring the prophetic word of God with purity. It's where the believer becomes cautious not to speak vanities, but you quietly wait for the anointing of the Lord upon your mouth as they did in the upper room. That's what happened in the upper room, a prayer revival broke out and they gave birth to a move of God that covered the known world. Now let us rise up and work diligently while it is day. Working the works of God, destroying the works of the devil. Let us march on to higher heights and deeper depths to declare the wondrous works of our God.

Chapter Overview

We can all be a little guilty of working too much or not enough at different times, and we can all identify at various points in our lives with each one of these little porkers. The point to keep close to the heart is that ultimately only what we do for Christ and his Kingdom will last, not just saying it is in His name but operating as He would operate under his Father's command in obedience to his will. Remember excellence in one's work comes when we study to show ourselves approved unto God. In this way we will find ourselves not given over to the shame associated with producing shoddy work in the Name of Christ.

This powerful principle can be applied to most anything we put our hands to, whether it is working to build a good relationship with someone, a family, a marriage, a business or a ministry. How we build will determine the outcome, this involves our motive as well as our efforts. Welcome the advice of the Holy Spirit in Christ, as he is the great architect of heaven and His wisdom will be the difference between building fast and building to last.

CHAPTER FOUR

THE NATURE OF THE WOLF

Whether you could identify with the Little Boy Who Cried Wolf, Little Red Riding Hood or the Three Little Pigs is not the issue. The real point is that the wolf is the same in each story. The stories may be fictional, but the wolf is very real. He is alive and preying upon unsuspecting believers at this very moment.

Let's examine the wolf further, because it does the believer no good to know that there is a wolf if he cannot be identified when we make first contact with him. It's not good enough to know where he is, but you must know who he is. His character largely identifies him. A wolf is a fierce animal that prowls at night and is especially destructive to sheep. They are cruel, but cowardly creatures, swift on their feet and strong enough to run with a sheep at full speed. The wolf is the dread of shepherds. They seclude themselves until dark among the rocks, then leap into the fold to seize their victim. The wolf first tears out the entrails and devours the heart, liver and lungs. It is important to remember when a wolf is on the prowl he travels alone.

Let's now look at what the word of God has to say about spiritual wolves and how to watch for them. The nature of a wolf is ravenous; he has a greedy hunger. Similarly, spiritual wolves are marked by their greedy natures, the more they see the more they want. They have unquenchable appetites and are rarely ever satisfied, and if so, it is momentarily.

In Jeremiah 5:6, the prophet speaks of the wolf as a spoiler, one who comes to injure and harm. These people leave you spiritually disfigured. Prolonged exposure to people with this spirit will bring about spiritual deterioration in your life or ministry. They have a way of reducing you. When you no longer serve a purpose for them, they move on to the next victim already hungry as they make the journey. In John 10:12, the wolf is revealed as one who not only eats, but also scatters the sheep. It doesn't matter how this spirit presents itself as being with you or for you, the end result will be a type of scattering amongst the flock. The wolf does not gather God's flock together except to choose his prey. Once he has isolated his victim, he then comes in for the kill and snatches that one away. These people come in to help strengthen your church and they leave with your members to start their own church.

Somehow, people always leave with them even if it's only one person. It may be a musician, a deacon or a young woman. It's always someone who has something to offer that they have a need for. The word instructs us to plant the people, the spirit of a wolf gathers from church to church and city to city. He preys on small ignorant groups or churches with little structure or no true doctrinal stability. Instead of truly feeding the sheep they only have the appearance of one who has come to feed them.

"Beware of false prophets, which come to you in sheep's clothing, but inwardly they are ravening wolves." - Matthew 7:15 KJV

This speaks of the duality of their personality. Outwardly, they appear to be humble and sincere but inwardly something malicious is underway. It is my personal opinion and experience that these types of people do operate out of a true duality of personality, two distinctly different minds in one person. These people have perfected an outward personality that is versed in all of the right things to say. They are skilled orators. They have worked very hard at perfecting an appropriate outward appearance, yet the inward man is unskilled and undeveloped. The outer appearance is confident and sincere. The inward person is insecure and untrustworthy. James says, this is the man that truly deceives only himself in the end. He hears and even knows, but simply will not do even what he expects from others.

"For if any be a hearer of the word, and not a doer, he is like unto a man beholding his natural face in a glass: for he beholdeth himself,

and goeth his way, and straightway forgetteth what manner of man he was." - James 1:23-24 KJV

All sheep are in danger of wolves but the wolf really is a cowardly creature. He doesn't act out in the open or the daylight, but he draws near to the flock hiding in the rock until he has chosen his prey. He watches for the weakest and identifies which sheep is slow and lagging behind. He is at heart a stalker, at the sight of nightfall, he seizes his victim and runs away. Likewise, in the church some have more of an appearance as potential victims than others do. Women more often than not appear to be easy victims, especially women in full-time ministry and leadership position who are not allowing their lives to be fully governed by the spirit of God. It's not hard to identify women who are wounded, lonely or just plain silly. Women who respond with giggly and giddy spiritual behavior at the first sight of attention. Women who sit in the congregation shopping for a mate instead of seeking the fullness of God's spirit. Sunday after Sunday, they entertain the attention of seducing spirits that move through the air filling their minds with lies. They lack the skill or discipline to cast these imaginations down. In their minds instead of being renewed to a position of strength and soundness, they become breeding grounds of deception. The least bit of attention is viewed as an opportunity to be swept off their feet, never to be lonely again, never to be responsible for themselves so they wait to be deceived. In Paul's writing to Timothy, he spoke of men's hearts in the last days and in this, he revealed the wolf's nature.

"This know also, that in the last days perilous times shall come. For men shall be lovers of their own selves, covetous, boasters, proud, blasphemers, disobedient to parents, unthankful, unholy, Without natural affection, trucebreakers, false accusers, incontinent, fierce, despisers of those that are good, traitors, heady, high-minded, lovers of pleasures more than lovers of God; having a form of godliness, but denying the power thereof: from such turn away. For of this sort are they which creep into houses, and lead captive silly women laden with sins, led away with divers lusts, ever learning, and never able to come to the knowledge of the truth." - 2 Timothy 3:1-7 KJV

Paul advised Timothy to admonish the church and to turn away from men of such character knowing that evil communication corrupt good manners. Paul didn't want this spirit spreading throughout the church. He further warns the church that out of this bunch were men who took pleasure in creeping into homes of silly women captivating them with their seducing charm and because of the sins and lusts that were laden in their hearts, they are the easiest of prey and are readily drawn away. The sad fact is that the church seems to have developed a tolerance for such people. We miss the mark when the same revivalist comes to our church every year and always leaves his mark on the young women, sometimes even leaving his offspring. We must re-examine the methods of some leaders especially the ones who travel the evangelistic circuits and repetitive conference goers.

Apostles and prophets who view single and widowed women as God's means of blessing them as they travel from city to city must be re-examined. They run up credit card bills, spend mortgage money and savings on suits, shoes, jewelry all in the name of furthering the gospel. We must be careful not to take on the nature of a wolf under the pretense of obtaining a blessing. Not every prophet is Elijah and not every woman is the widow of Zarephath. We know that giving is a blessing to all who participate in it, but we also know that there are those who come only to serve themselves.

The Apostle Paul said, "Now as Jannes and Jambres withstood Moses, so do these also resist the truth: men of corrupt minds, reprobate concerning the faith." - 2 Timothy 3:8 KJV

This is not to say there are not true men and women of God ministering under the divine unction of the Holy Ghost. The fact of the matter is that the counterfeit does exist and this type of conduct in the church hinders the move of God. They rape and weaken the flock leaving them wounded and untrusting toward leadership. It is the enemy's intention to corrupt and infiltrate the ranks with His own hand picked mercenaries. He knows it takes time for God to masterfully make the real thing, true apostles, prophets, evangelists, pastors and teachers. True men and women of God who will teach the uncompromising gospel.

We must realize that the wolf nature appeals to the impatience in all of us. It knows many of us are weary of waiting on God even to the point of believing and receiving a lie. As leaders, we must take heed to wholeheartedly attend to the scriptures in a vigilant and diligent manner.

"For I have not shunned to declare unto you all the counsel of God. Take heed therefore unto yourselves, and to all the flock, over which the Holy Ghost hath made you overseers, to feed the church of God, which he hath purchased with his own blood. For I know this, that after my departing shall grievous wolves enter in among you, not sparing the flock." - Acts 20:27-29

These deplorable personalities have no care for an unsuspecting flock. Paul did not stop there, he went on to say,

"Also, of your own selves shall men arise, speaking perverse things, to draw away disciples after them. Therefore watch, and remember, that by the space of three years I ceased not to warn every one night and day with tears." - Acts 20:30-31 KJV

This ever-present danger so concerned Paul that he spent three years teaching and warning the church of such intruders even amongst themselves. (Acts 20:32) Jude exhorts us to earnestly contend for the faith because there are men that creep in unaware.
He said;

"Woe unto them! For they have gone in the way of Cain, and ran greedily after the error of Balaam for reward, and perished in the gainsaying of Core. These are spots in your feasts of charity, when they feast with you, feeding themselves without fear: clouds they are without water, carried about of winds; trees whose fruit withereth, without fruit, twice dead, plucked up by the roots; raging waves of the sea, foaming out of their own shame; wandering stars, to whom is reserved the blackness of darkness forever." - Jude 11-13 KJV

This is a very descriptive passage of scripture. It dramatically pin points some of the characteristics of someone with the spirit of a wolf operating in their lives. They have gone the way of Cain, who consumed with envy and jealousy took on the spirit of a murderer when he killed his brother in a fit of rage. And greed for gain was the sin that led Balaam to err. God is coming for a church without spot or blemish. Jude refers to these type of people as 'spots in your feast' (vs.12). Irreverent, disrespectful, clouds without water - they look full, they are swollen with many words, but they leave your presence and you are still dry and thirsty. Trees whose fruit withereth – the fruit they seem to produce doesn't remain, it withers and dies, they remain fruitless, and there is an evident trail of bareness behind them. It says out of their shame is wandering, there is a lack of structure and they are not submissive to real authority.

Verse. 8 in Jude calls them 'filthy dreamers" who defile the flesh. There is a clear pattern and these persons are not very hard to identify. They are usually powerfully persuasive, very charismatic, charming, full of appeal on the outside, attractive, lovable people full of personality. They are often so likeable that it causes you to second-guess your own unction as to what else is operating behind the scene. When the Holy Spirit exposes different areas of their identity, instead of addressing these issues, we tend to overlook them as mistakes or we keep giving them another chance. Jude warns us because they can seize the admiration of a whole congregation. But they are mockers who walk after their own ungodly lust. The Apostle Peter said they 'shall utterly perish in their own corruption." (2 Peter 2:12 KJV) Peter is also very descriptive about their motive, which is to make merchandise of you. They are presumptuous and self-willed.

"The Lord knoweth how to deliver the godly out of temptation, and to reserve the unjust unto the day of judgment to be punished:" - 2 Peter 2:9 KJV

"Do not be deceived; God is not mocked: for whatsoever a man soweth, that shall he also reap." - Galatians 6:7 KJV

For this reason, Matthew records a conversation Jesus had with his disciples and he warns them, "Behold, I send you forth as sheep in the midst of wolves: be ye therefore wise as serpents, and harmless as doves." - Matthew 10:16 KJV

In addition, Paul encourages Timothy (and us) with these words:

"Yea, and all that will live godly in Christ Jesus shall suffer persecution. But evil men and seducers shall wax worse and worse, deceiving, and being deceived. But continue in the things which thou hast learned and hast been assured of, knowing of whom thou hast learned them; and that from a child thou hast known the Holy scriptures, which are able to make thee wise unto salvation through faith which is in Christ Jesus.

All scripture is given by inspiration of God, and is profitable for doctrine, for reproof, for correction, for instruction in righteousness: that the man of God may be perfect, thoroughly furnished unto all good works." - 2 Timothy 3:12-17 KJV

Chapter Overview

There is no place in the Kingdom of God for preaching anything other than the word of God. Preaching catchy phrases and whimsical clichés will not produce the manifested power necessary to destroy the yokes of bondage or produce the liberty to set the captives free. Men and Women of God must persevere and remain steadfast in the love of God. Preaching for entertainment value or acceptance is fruitless and does not benefit or increase the believer who relies on the word of God to sustain spiritual life, the gospel must reflect the words and ways of Christ. It must come with reproof, rebuke when necessary and exhortation with all long suffering not compromising the words of Christ.

We are already living in times where sound doctrine is not welcomed in many so-called Christian circles or it is so watered down with the doctrine of devils that it will make even the healthiest believer sick to the stomach. This environment will attract the wolf nature and expose innocent souls to the predatory ways of individuals who open themselves up to this spirit because of greed and lust for power.

Five-fold ministry gifts must come together in unity and love, functioning effectively to cast a spiritual net over the their regions. This corporate working of gifts will discourage those open to the wolf nature from maturing into a full-blown predator, and will drive this deceitful spirit away from the flock. The absence of such unity or integrity of the word will certainly attract wolves among us.

"Preach the word; be instant in season, out of season; reprove, rebuke, exhort with all longsuffering and doctrine. For the time will come when they will not endure sound doctrine; but after their own lusts shall they heap to themselves teachers, having itching ears." - 2 Timothy 4:2-3 KJV

CHAPTER FIVE

MY ENCOUNTER, ESPECIALLY FOR WOMEN

On November 27,1996, after having survived my own personal encounter with the spirit of a wolf, a friend in the gospel was anointed by the Holy Ghost to share these words with me. Leaders and overseers of God's precious flock must adhere to this plea:

"Now I beseech you, brethren, mark them which cause divisions and offenses contrary to the doctrine which ye have learned; and avoid them. For they that are such serve not our Lord Jesus Christ, but their own belly; and by good words and fair speeches deceive the hearts of the simple. For your obedience is come abroad unto all men. I am glad therefore on your behalf: but yet I would have you wise unto that which is good, and simple concerning evil. And the God of peace shall bruise Satan under your feet shortly. The grace of our Lord Jesus Christ be with you. Amen." - Romans 16:17-20 KJV

The one thing that I have learned is you don't start off as a wolf. It is a spirit that attaches itself to the character and nature of a person. The enemy lies in wait, identifying the weaknesses and unrepented attributes in our nature that make us compatible with the nature of this spirit. This spirit usually attaches itself to men who have been wounded and broken by life's experiences. They are filled with rejection and insecurity, causing them to be inwardly cowards. The wolf serves as a protective covering and this spirit builds them with a false sense of masculinity and security. Many have been either abused or abandoned by maternal role models, So there is an indwelling hatred toward women, yet a genuine need for their assistance, attention and approval.

These people would probably receive true deliverance if they were dealt with in true righteousness, allowing the spirit in operation to be exposed in its early stages. We must be careful how we govern our actions and attitudes so that this spirit is not found operating in our lives. If it is found, it must be immediately repented of and cast down or it will overtake you as a prey and then use you to prey on the Lord's flock.

The bible speaks of the enemy as a thief, who comes to steal, kill and destroy. The wolf is characterized as this type of enemy. The wolf is a thief, and he has a desire for what is not his. He knows it doesn't belong to him, which explains why he is sneaking to get it. He never operates in the open and avoids being exposed by the light of God's word. He hides behind the ignorance of people and their inability to discern and distinguish the true traits of his character. He even hides himself in the word of God manipulating, perpetrating and cultivating to his own personal devices as an ambassador of Christ.

Many young and old women in the church need to be delivered from what I once was bound by. I call it "The Knight in Shining Armor Syndrome". When women are confronted with their own personal weaknesses and insecurities, instead of being strong in the Lord and in the power of His might, we whimper and cry out for someone to rescue us. I had to learn the hard way that there are many battles God will not rescue you from. Some things you just have to learn how to face, fight and overcome. I wanted someone to rescue me from my own personal battles; I wanted someone to take care of me so I would be free from taking care of myself. Gradually as I surrendered myself into the strong able hands of my knight, I was losing the things God had placed in my hands. Over time, I eventually lost everything except my life and the personal presence of the Holy Spirit. Like Israel, in all of my whoring after other God's, he had not forsaken me, but I had been allowing a man to replace him.

Six to eight months into my marriage the love of my life turned into the nightmare of my dreams. The wolf himself took great pleasure in informing me that I belonged to him lock, stock and license. The war was on and I knew I couldn't run from this encounter. My own ignorance and disobedience brought me to this point and there was no one who could help me except God. War erupted in the church and war erupted in my home. He swore to break me like a wild animal that needed taming.

My only skilled weaponry for dealing with this type of man was with the nature of my old man. When we take on the righteousness of God, our carnal weapons don't work the same way for us as we experienced in the world. When we try to use carnal weapons in the kingdom of God, they backfire on us. The devil knows this and he counts on his ability to keep us warring in the flesh. He knows frustrations come when we don't know how to battle old demons with spiritual weapons so he is right there to arm us with the nature of our old man. He knows it leads to destruction and defeat. Instead my God used this personal encounter to teach me how to fight a good fight. He taught me how to know he was with me even when it didn't appear that he was with me. He taught me how to distinguish his voice from every other voice. I learned that the weapons of my warfare are not carnal, but mighty through God to the pulling down of strongholds. I learned how to wait on God. After having loss everything: family, children, friends, status, stature, respect, the church and time; my confidence ailing, my strength failing, all I could do was believe that God had not forgotten me.

One night the spirit of the Lord awakened me out of my sleep and this is what he spoke, "Your days of weeping and reaping have come to an end." I knew deliverance was at my door. I didn't know how it was coming and I didn't care because I was ready. The next day just like my knight came he suddenly left. This personal encounter, this intimate relationship touched and changed my life forever.

When it comes to dealing with the nature and characteristics of a wolf, the people involved and the circumstances may be different but one thing remains the same. This one spirit seeks to destroy us and everything good in our lives.

A wolf is a wolf is a wolf; in a dress, a suit or sheep's clothing, he is still a wolf. I know that God loves us and he will not cripple us in any way. He won't intercept every battle just because we cry, nor will he fight every battle for us. Because he has equipped us with spiritual gifts; given us his spirit, assured us of the upcoming victory and sent us out to cry out aloud and sound the alarm when there are wolves in the house.

He tells us to "Be strong in the Lord and in the power of his might". - Ephesians 6:10 KJV

We have a good shepherd, So, fight the good fight!

As I look back over my own experiences, I realized a few things about myself. First of all, I was very arrogant in a very subtle way. Quiet arrogance can be far worse than full in your face arrogance. Mine was tucked neatly in my own heart away from any watchful eyes, but I can't say I myself was oblivious to it. I was aware of the condescending behaviors and thoughts all safely hidden behind good works and deeds. I knew of the hidden lust in my heart and I hid it even deeper and covered it from any suspecting eye, I was ashamed of it but I had no one I thought I could trust with such incriminating information about myself. I did not understand spiritual root systems or demonic strongholds, where you can be saved but not completely set free.

Pride was definitely a doorway that the enemy used to overtake me in a series of calculated steps and my God, how strategic those steps were now that I look back at the whole encounter and the events leading up to it.

They went as follows: Steps one through Ten

1. Denial
2. Imbalance
3. Wounded
4. Unforgiveness
5. Defiance in the face of attack
6. Refusal to take time off to heal
7. Showed no humility in the face of temptation
8. Continue to flirt with temptation after becoming aware of it
9. Ignoring the danger of the confrontation- proceeding alone
10. The fall and the fallout

...The wolf and I alone in one calculated encounter, the damage done, my life is destroyed.

Most go through these steps whether they realize it or not. You may even find yourself in there somewhere, I went through all ten.

I survived, only by God's Grace. I lived to tell the story and to warn others, this was the arrow of the enemy straight to the heart. It was intended not just to kill but to destroy!

It had the power to steal all joy, kill all hope, destroy all involved – the guilty and the innocent. Ten diabolical steps and it was over, I kept telling myself I was okay and I was in control. What a lie from the pit of Hell. I was certainly not okay and definitely not in control, but I was deceived and that is what Satan was counting on. I denied the truth of what God was showing me about myself.

Step one, I denied my need for deliverance in the deepest parts of my soul. Step two, I covered up a lot of the painful bondage attached to my past by being consumed with the work of the kingdom instead of the work of his Holiness through the Holy Spirit. I was at the church all the time when I wasn't there, I was somewhere else. It was the fall of 1989 I came home from work one day to find my sister-in-law in my bed she had been having an affair with my husband and quickly went through steps three, four, five and six.

The groundwork was laid and now everything was primed for step seven. I was faced with my temptation about three months later when he (the person who would bring the wolf to my door) showed up on the last night of a spring revival. My soon to be knight in shining armor- it was as if a realm opened up to us both and in this place, we stood on a great battlefield, two lone warriors both wounded but still fierce. We examined each other as though we were sizing up an opponent. There was something strangely seductive about this encounter and each one was intrigued by the mystery around the wounds and the armament of the other after what seemed like a long period of time, but in reality, it had been just seconds.

We decided to be friends rather than foes and the window closed.

We were back in the fellowship hall with everyone else, having cake and coffee. Neither one of us acknowledged what had happened, but we knew the next week he returned to continue the revival, another week and the foundation had been secured firmly with step seven. He would call me a few months later in trouble and I would go to his aid. I knew what it was like to be alone in a battle and need help. This was the beginning of the summer of 1989. Physically, I was stronger, mentally he was stronger, emotionally we were both a wreck, but together we would keep each other alive to fight another day. I did not see it when it was happening, but hindsight is a great teacher. I was becoming his idol and he was becoming my god. We were leaning more on each other than anyone else including the Holy Spirit with each passing day.

Step Eight would not happen overnight, it would be over a year later. The enemy of our souls is filled with cunning wiles and he knew in the beginning we were both still too suspicious of the other so he baited us using our own arrogant confidence against us, until it was too late. We had been too close too many times and nothing bad had happened, there was a fierce attraction to do every battle together. We marveled at how much more effective we were together just for the sake of the kingdom. About nine months in we were aware of this strong chemistry between us, but again our prideful arrogance gave us permission to proceed. Two mighty warriors, neither would be the first to admit any form of weakness. Certainly not this kind, so we continued from one battlefield to another as our personal lives unraveled and fell apart. We were both too blind to see the coming fallout or the years of devastation that would affect everyone we knew and people we had not even met yet. By the winter of 1990, after his marriage had fallen apart and so had my own, he decided to return to Chicago to be with his father and hopefully recover, but we could not stand the thought of being away from each other. Feeding our deceitfulness, he invited me to do a service in Chicago. At this point, I had neither strength nor integrity to say no, knowing full well we were both using this as an occasion to see each other and I returned from Chicago carrying more than luggage.

I was carrying his Son. "What a wicked web we weave when we first plan to deceive." In January I missed my cycle and by February

44

he had returned now keeping to the nature of a warrior, we were broken and fallen, but we were together and we thought that was enough to get us through, but it wasn't as we would eventually find out how wrong we were. The fallout would include both our families, all of our children and both ministries, the ripple would extend across the country and back. Like the aftermath of a great earthquake the spiritual ground broke and shook underneath the weight of our sin.

The Lord had warned me that his presence would depart from me if I did anything to the life of this child who belonged to him. The sin may have been ours, but the soul of the child belonged to the Lord. He let me know I would lose everything in the long run, but through it all he would be with me. It would be many years before my obedience would reveal its benefits. I remember the Lord telling me that many others had been in this same situation but had refused to submit to Him in the midst of it, instead choosing to cover their sinful tracks and move on as though God had not seen them.

My warrior and I married, determined to stick it out together, ride or die. No soldier abandons the other in the thick of the battle −not until the enemy turned the battle on us. In the confusion, and the derangement of it all we were back to where we met, in that vision in the fellowship hall. Two suspicious warriors on the battlefield, a wasteland of destruction. This time when we looked at each other in our self- imposed distress and desperation for survival we became foe instead of friend, it was going to be kill, or be killed and each had a decision to make. I loved him and it was this weakness that exposed me to the death blow. Just as he had come, he was now gone again. He married someone else without me even knowing it had happened. I still could forgive him if he came to his senses, and after five years he would return to drive the dagger in the jugular by stealing the kids from under my unsuspecting eyes. That was the final blow for me. It would be the words of our son that would cause me to surrender to the death. He called me on the phone one day as his father and I were in the heat of battle with tears he said to me, "Mommy please for my sake, Stop fighting with Dad". I was done. If I didn't give up this fight my children would be destroyed in the wake of our fury. If I stopped the pain would kill me, but they would be okay. Surely, as God has told me I had lost everything including the will to fight.

I think that was the day I truly realized my flesh had to die. If we were going to survive, I would need to trust God.
I spent the next three years walking like a dead man, only God and his presence remained. If only I had known that this death would be the key to my liberty and increased life in Christ, I believe I would have died sooner.

The next chapter is written in memory of the wolf that left me with the knowledge to set the captives free. I pray that today I will help someone to identify if a wolf is stalking them. Don't run, just turn and take a stand because he's already been defanged.

If you are ready to heal from the wounds that have been inflicted on your soul, join me on the journey to a place called "Whole".

CHAPTER SIX

THE JOURNEY TO A PLACE CALLED WHOLE

"We can't make the journey to a place called "Whole" without discovering the Path of Restoration"

The path of restoration should lead to completeness or wholeness. It should not be a revolving cycle of needing to be healed -over and over again in the same areas of your life. Often times healing becomes no more than bandaging or scabbing old unhealed wounds. Because we tend to be so impatient, we look for quick-fix solutions where bandages (cover up) our wounds. The other quick fix is scabbing. We have a minimum amount of human patience, but no endurance for Godly long-suffering, so we check out at the first sign of healing without understanding that many wounds run much deeper than we realize or are willing to admit. We walk away with a scab on our emotions, unconscious of the deeper cut until it's reopened by a new encounter.

True restoration consists of repairing, curing, re-establishing, and giving back. It's taking something weak and making is strong again. Sometimes that even means making it over. This is when we need a trip to the potter's house (Jeremiah 18:1-4).

Restoration is never complete until it brings us to a place called whole. Whole is when we are sound; sound in mind, healthy in spirit and healed in the soul. It means we are now intact, in entirety in spirit, soul and body. There is no dysfunction in our being. It doesn't mean we stop making mistakes, but it does mean we invite the opportunity to examine our decisions even if we discover we are to blame. It is a place of responsibility not avoidance.

Many times, we avoid the journey to wholeness because we are afraid of looking at the darkness in our own souls. It can be like a black hole, we don't know where it begins or ends, and we don't know what's in it so we avoid it all together. It's usually only when our pain has become greater than our fear that we are ready to be made whole. This is where we must be honest in answering the question, "do you want to be made whole?".

It is a fact that the journey to whole can often seem to be even more painful than the experience that wounded us. When we are hurting, we often feel like victims. We may think it's not our fault that we've been hurt. We just want our pain validated, we want satisfaction and assurance that someone pays for what has happened to us. However, on the real road to whole we can discover that we are in fact guilty of something.

Sometimes we are guilty of negligence in attending to the affairs of our own soul or we may be guilty of being ignorant of the enemy's devices. In any event, it is hard to play the blame game without pinning some of it on our own backs.

"Healing is a process. Restoration is a path on the journey. WHOLE is a destination; a position and place I pray that is a goal for all of us. Most of us need a little assistance getting started".

Once you start the journey, having a sense of direction is important to help you stay on track. To help, I've outlined seven steps that are essential in your journey. I had to submit to the discipline of the Holy Spirit and walk with Him through my death-valley.

These next steps did not happen overnight or all at once, it was over many years. I had to submit myself daily to the care of the Holy Spirit. I had to choose to walk with Him, in His truth every day and allow Him to expose the inner parts of my own soul to me, as the time passed. Each day was a day to walk in truth, then more truth, then greater truth. Sometimes obedience was painful, but each time I looked back I knew there was no other place for me except forward and deeper into him and his will, his love, and his Kingdom.

The Seven Steps to Restoration

Step One: Accept Responsibility for Your Own Soul (Even if it is wounded or broken)

"Let no man say when he is tempted, I am tempted of God: for God cannot be tempted with evil, neither tempteth he any man: but every man is tempted, when he is drawn away of his own lust, and enticed. Then when lust hath conceived, it bringeth forth sin: and sin, when it is finished, bringeth forth death." - James 1:13-15 KJV

When we are tempted and enticed it is by our own inner desires, these desires can be for a person, place, position or thing. Many of us will stop short of nothing to get the object of our desires, no matter what the consequences. Because while we are being seduced, we are also blinded and unable or unwilling to consider the consequences. It is only when the pain of dying invades our experience and as death is manifesting to our soul we begin to pay attention. Death is presented as a loss and when we lose something, we feel the pain of our losses.

However, James says: "Therefore, submit to God. Resist the devil and he will flee from you. Draw near to God and He will draw near to you. Cleanse your hands, you sinners; and purify your hearts, you double-minded. Lament and mourn and weep! Let your laughter be turned into mourning and your joy to gloom. Humble yourselves in the sight of the Lord, and He will lift you up." - James 4:7-10 NKJV

In this scripture, we find strength on the battlefield of temptation. It is not a sin to be tempted-we are all tempted. We sin when we are drawn away in our temptation and seduced by the desires in our own hearts. When we draw near to God, He helps us to see through the eyes of the Spirit. We must be open to the cleansing work of the Holy Spirit to lovingly assist us in looking at the darkness that resides in our hearts. Often these hidden snares continue to entangle us in the yoke of bondage. It is here that we lament, mourn and weep over what we see. It is here that our laughter turns into mourning and our joy to gloom. At this point, it is very necessary to humble ourselves in the sight of the Lord. Without humility, many of us would not go any further nor would we be willing to look any closer. Here in true humility the Lord is able to lift us up so we can see what He sees. Seduction quickly loses its appeal and sin loses its grip when it's uncovered for us to see the ugly stain it leaves on our soul.

Step Two: Sin No More

"When Jesus had raised Himself up and saw no one but the woman, He said to her, "Woman, where are those accusers of yours?" Has no one condemned you? She said, "No one, Lord." And Jesus said to her, "Neither do I condemn you; go and sin no more." John 8:10-11 NKJV

There is liberty in Christ; we can freely bring our sins to Him without fear or condemnation. Not only are we free from his condemnation, but He will not allow anyone to condemn us in his sight without first exposing their own sins. Our accusers find no justification in their actions against us when standing before the Lord.

If you truly desire to be made whole, you must first be willing to Sin No More. Enter into the renewed mind of no longer desiring to be a habitual intentional sinner without true remorse This in no way means we are to attempt this on our own. Jesus grants the desires of our heart when we have a sincere desire to live holy. Then our desire to please the Lord is granted through deliverance from the sin that has imprisoned us. Now we can go from this point with a clean heart and a pure desire to SIN NO MORE.

Step Three: Initiate and Accept Continual Cleansing

This must become a daily part of your life not to hide from God as Adam did. Instead, come openly to God confessing daily and initiating the forgiveness you need to remain cleansed.

Step Four: Submit to the Discipline of the Spirit

"Now no chastening seems to be joyful for the present, but painful; nevertheless, afterward it yields the peaceable fruit of righteousness to those who have been trained by it." - Hebrews 12:11 NKJV

If you allow the Holy Spirit access to the seat of your will, He will teach you how to discipline your spirit. He will assist you in the spiritual technique of restraining your soul. Initially, the process can be painful. It is confining and full of restraints. If you remember being an adolescent, it is very much like being on punishment. However, the benefits of this process far out-weighs any of its discomforts.

The fruit of any discipline is maturity and growth. Therefore, the purpose of this step is to open the eyes of your understanding so you can see things as God sees them for you. Over time, you will mature and grow to a place where you are thoroughly furnished (equipped) to do a good work.

The part of this step that can be most discouraging is that it does not happen overnight. The discipline of the Spirit will develop your spiritual life until the doctrine of Jesus Christ abides in your soul. Where there is doctrine in your soul, you can endure trials and persecutions without having your soul suffer damage.

Step Five: Flee from Lust and Greed

"And having food and clothing, with these we shall be content. But those who desire to be rich fall into temptation and a snare, and into many foolish and harmful lusts which drown men in destruction and perdition. For the love of money is a root of all kinds of evil, for which some have strayed from the faith in their greediness, and pierced themselves through with many sorrows. But you, O man of God, flee these things and pursue righteousness, godliness, faith, love, patience, gentleness." - 1 Timothy 6:8-11 NKJV

Lust and greed for material gain has destroyed many great nations whose appetite was never satisfied, as long as there was more to accumulate. The enemy of our souls is a great strategist, seizing every window of opportunity we afford him into our lives. For this reason, resisting his temptation is not enough. We are warned in 1 Timothy 6 to FLEE, RUN, TAKE FLIGHT to escape the foolish desires that lie in wait to snare the unsuspecting soul.

With this in mind, you must never lose touch with how easily an unnoticeable temptation can become a death trap. In addition, you cannot just flee, to do so without pursuing something else in its place means you will always be fleeing and never arriving. This leaves you in a position of even greater risk. The position of being overtaken in other ways. It is not until you pursue the life of Christ with all diligence (not wavering in what it is that you truly desire) that you arrive at righteous, godly, faithful, living full of love, patience and gentleness of heart. It is here, in this pursuit to become like Christ that we must fight the good fight. After having done so, we are now able to focus in and appreciate the present benefits of laying hold to eternal life.

Step Six: Desire Obedience

"For though we walk in the flesh, we do not war according to the flesh. For the weapons of our warfare are not carnal but mighty in God for pulling down strongholds, casting down arguments and every high thing that exalts itself against the knowledge of God, bringing every thought into captivity to the obedience of Christ, and being ready to punish all disobedience when you obedience is fulfilled." - 2 Corinthians 10:3-6 NKJV

At this point in your walk with God , there must be a desire for obedience. It is here that you must wholeheartedly trust and depend upon the word of God to both sustain and direct your daily walk with God. Here as believers, we look with great anticipation to serve God with an obedient heart. Always ready to punish any thought of disobedience by cutting it off and casting it down. Fulfilled obedience will produce the mature Christ life necessary to defeat Satan and walk upright before God. Here. you are deemed worthy or your vocation. This is the foundation upon which step seven is laid. It will take courage to wake up and do this every day, but if you look to God and lean into his grace you will find the courage to do it each and every day.

Step Seven: No Lack

"The Lord is my shepherd; I shall not want." - Psalms 23:1 NKJV

When you allow God to shepherd you, you are not driven like cattle by your desires. You are led like sheep through your complete and unquestionable reliance on a Holy God. A good shepherd – one who knows how to care for your soul. Under his watchful eye, you are free to graze upon His word and grow in His grace. No harm will come to the soul that trusts in him.

Here there is no lack, no need to want what He has not provided for. You trust His provision is all you need. You will not hear or follow the voice of another. His son, the only begotten of the Father, Jesus Christ is the bishop of your soul. Under His watchful eye, you are blessed and the blessings of God make you rich and add no sorrow. With confidence in Him, you are free from worry though your natural bodies may be afflicted and your physical man persecuted. You fear no evil, for he is with you through it all and in His word, you are comforted.

The treachery of the enemy cannot lay hold on the spirit that is completely submitted to the shepherding care of our Lord. Spirit, soul and body we say, 'I'm Yours Lord, Completely Yours."

"Each day was a day to walk in truth, then more truth, then greater truth. Sometimes obedience was painful, but each time I looked back I knew there was no other place for me except forward and deeper into him and his will, his love, and his Kingdom".

Chapter Overview

Many people, especially women, seek religious association and find their way into the four walls of man-made structures that we call "The Church". Here they expect to find solace, comfort, refuge, sanctuary and acceptance. They see this as a place to be healed, rescued and protected. However, often they discover it is an unprotected hunting ground. A place where more heartache and sorrow will be inflicted upon their already fragile souls. A place where wolves and predators gather because it is a prime and plentiful place to hunt wounded prey. A place where a loving Creator receives the blame for the corruption perpetrated by unfaithful leaders, who lie and deceive in His name. It was only when my own soul laid mangled and broken, no longer necessary to the physical (church) institution, no longer profitable to its' cause that I ventured onto a journey to a place called whole and discovered a universal entity; a church without walls or borders. A church invisible and unseen by the naked eye. I found it in the compassionate touch of a stranger, the kindness of a heart without a hidden motive or agenda.

I discovered that love is not confined to a physical thing or even a person. It is the divine presence of a concerned Creator whose church is in the fields of humanity unable to be identified with the naked eye. Yet, within this universal and invisible church there will remain a man-made structure that has been erected to capture the essence of His glorious kingdom and if we are to present an invisible God, and his kingdom to a people who do not know Him, there must be order in the church.

This order must consist of spiritual governmental authority as well as civil obedience and order. There must be a demand for purity and excellence placed upon every person who steps up to answer the call of God on his or her life. This type of order is only established where Christ is both acknowledged and accepted as the head and sole figure of authority over His church, which is always and shall be "the Body of Christ".

Realistically, one would have to concede where Christ is not the head of the church, that church - is not His. This is both a figurative and literal statement. We, as individual believers, are members of his body. In our hearts, His kingdom resides. If He is not the head and king of that kingdom then, that kingdom - is not His. Where He is king, He is the ruling authority and His government is without reproach.

As ministers and stewards of the gospel of Jesus Christ, we must attend wholeheartedly to the house of God. Because it is the visible house that reflects the glory of the invisible God. The wall that separates the church from the world must never be without its watchmen. Individuals who have been divinely appointed by God to pierce through the darkness of this worldly system and warn the shepherds of impending danger.

We must cry aloud and spare not the soul that would otherwise be destroyed in our silence. The shepherds must be willing to examine and judge themselves under the microscope of God's word, where they will be shepherds after God's own heart or shepherds who have devised their own plan for leading God's people. The human oversight of God's house cannot remain confined within our four-walled structures. It must extend itself back into the communities in which we live. Bishops, Apostles and Overseers can't afford to see themselves at a point in which they have arrived, but in a position in which they have just begun.

Remember, when our own spirit has developed to a position of maturity it is disciplined under the direction of the Holy Spirit. The doctrine of Christ is engraved on the heart allowing us to walk worthy of the vocation to which they are called. Then we can begin to grasp the depth and weight of the responsibility of leadership. This authority is not limited, restrained or confined within four walls; it is established in the fields of humanity. It reaches into the highways and byways. This voice of authority compels men and women to answer the call of the spirit and come. Indeed, they will come: the who-so-ever will, they will hear the gospel of his Kingdom and respond with faith.

They are the lame, the blind, the weak, the weary and the sick. All coming to be healed and delivered from their pains, to be protected and shepherded under God's watchful care. We must attend to God's flock carefully and prayerfully. This responsibility cannot rest in the hands of the novice apprentice looking for practice. Let us, as leaders, search our souls with all diligence that we may be found worthy to man the post which we have been assigned.

The wolf is alive and well and he may be on his way to your house. The only question is: Are You Ready?

CHAPTER SEVEN

THE SEVEN STEPS TO RESTORATION

These steps are directly from the previous chapter and can be used as a study outline or a reference to chart your own progress on your road to recovery. There are seven essential steps in your journey. Record your own thoughts and those of the Spirit as you walk through these important steps toward wholeness. Take your time and meditate in prayer on each of these steps.

Step One: Accept Responsibility for Your Own Soul (Even if it is wounded or broken.)

"Let no man say when he is tempted, I am tempted of God: for God cannot be tempted with evil, neither tempteth he any man: but every man is tempted, when he is drawn away of his own lust, and enticed. Then when lust hath conceived, it bringeth forth sin: and sin, when it is finished, bringeth forth death." - James 1:13-15 KJV

Have you accepted responsibility?

_____
_____
_____
_____
_____
_____
_____
_____
_____
_____
_____
_____
_____

"Therefore, submit to God. Resist the devil and he will flee from you. Draw near to God and He will draw near to you. Cleanse your hands, you sinners; and purify your hearts, you double-minded. Lament and mourn and weep! Let your laughter be turned into mourning and your joy to gloom. Humble yourselves in the sight of the Lord, and He will lift you up." - James 4:7-10 NKJV

Step Two: Sin No More

"When Jesus had raised Himself up and saw no one but the woman, He said to her, "Woman, where are those accusers of yours?" Has no one condemned you? She said, "No one, Lord." And Jesus said to her, "Neither do I condemn you; go and sin no more." - John 8:10-11 NKJV

Do you have the willingness of heart to stop sinning or whatever you are doing to hurt you or others?

_____
_____
_____
_____
_____
_____
_____
_____
_____
_____
_____

Step Three: Initiate and Accept Continual Cleansing

This must become a daily part of your life not to hide from God as Adam did. Instead, come openly to God confessing daily and initiating the forgiveness you need to remain cleansed. David prayer a powerful prayer in Psalms 51 initiating cleansing in his own life. David asked the Lord to wash him from his iniquity and cleanse him from his sin. He initiates four deep needs for the soul.

1. To be purged
2. To be washed
3. To be made to hear joy and gladness
4. To be restored and upheld through a clean heart and a renewed spirit

How willing are you to walk in continuous this cleansing?

_____
_____
_____
_____
_____
_____
_____
_____
_____
_____
_____

Step Four: Submit to the Discipline of the Holy Spirit

"Now no chastening seems to be joyful for the present, but painful; nevertheless, afterward it yields the peaceable fruit of righteousness to those who have been trained by it." - Hebrews 12:11 NKJV

What can you identify in prayer that may be stopping you from submitting to his discipline?

_____
_____
_____
_____
_____
_____
_____
_____
_____
_____

Step Five: Flee from Lust and Greed

And having food and clothing, with these we shall be content. But those who desire to be rich fall into temptation and a snare, and into many foolish and harmful lusts which drown men in destruction and perdition. For the love of money is a root of all kinds of evil, for which some have strayed from the faith in their greediness, and pierced themselves through with many sorrows. But you, O man of God, flee these things and pursue righteousness, godliness, faith, love, patience, gentleness.- 1 Timothy 6:8-11 NKJV

I will be the first one to tell you that step five is easier said than done, but we have what it takes in Christ to persevere into this step and be successful. Fleeing and pursuing is a collaborative effort and these steps must be done in conjunction with the other.

Can you identify the areas in your life where you see evidence of lust or greed?

_____
_____
_____
_____
_____
_____
_____
_____
_____
_____
_____

Step Six: Desire Obedience

"For though we walk in the flesh, we do not war according to the flesh. For the weapons of our warfare are not carnal but mighty in God for pulling down strongholds, casting down arguments and every high thing that exalts itself against the knowledge of God, bringing every thought into captivity to the obedience of Christ, and being ready to punish all disobedience when your obedience is fulfilled." - 2 Corinthians 10:3-6 NKJV

What are the areas of your walk with God where your desire greater obedience?

_____

_____

_____

_____

_____

_____

_____

_____

_____

_____

Step Seven: No Lack

"The Lord is my shepherd; I shall not want." - Psalms 23:1 NKJV

He is the God who provides and He is all sufficient in His care for us. His provisions are daily and non- stop- they are continuous as we need them. We don't have to beg Him as His willingness to care for us will always supersede our need to be cared for. From Manna in the wilderness to the widow's total provision and continual supply, He is God and He is able. So able is He, that it exceeds our finite minds going far above our ability to ask. We see needs as being temporal God seeing them as eternal provides exceedingly and abundantly above what we know to ask.

Arm yourselves with these truths and remain both content and ready, watch and pray that you do not enter into temptation.

For the spirit is willing, but the flesh is weak!

Can you list all the things you have to be grateful for as you consider the provisions of the Lord in your life?

_____

_____

_____

_____

CHAPTER EIGHT

FINAL CHAPTER OVERVIEW

Here is the fruit, as I have learned a few things at the feet of Jesus. In these 30 plus years the Holy Spirit has given me a proper education that I relate to through the eyes of the Apostle Paul, a chief among sinners like myself.

The Apostle Paul introduces to us the great and weighty spiritual advantage of the pure word of God and the life it produces in us when we trust in it. He encounters his naysayers and spiritual opponents- not with hatred, but with truth spoken in love. I was in my early years of ministry when I heard the Spirit within me speak of the Apostle Paul the first time. I had read the bible every day, but this day I was at the church in fasting and prayer seeking the Lord for direction when I heard within me, "You will be like the Apostle Paul" it caught my attention as I was in a quiet, meditative place. I began to wonder, what was it about this particular Apostle that I would be like? Then the next thing I hear is that in the last days true men and women of God will be accused of heresy. The Holy Spirit was warning me that at some point in my life like the Apostle Paul I would be persecuted for telling the truth. Thank God persecution is easier if you start from the position of being dead in Christ. What was even more startling was that the truth would not be welcomed by many who say they are believers.

That conversation in prayer was over 30 years ago and I have lived to see how much of what the Lord was sharing with me that day is not only possible, but much has come to pass. The Apostle Paul had every right to defend himself against his own accusers but he refused to stoop to such a level, choosing rather to glory in the work of Christ in his own life. I must confess that this has been a great challenge in my own walk with the Lord. I mean, it is human to want to defend yourself, to speak up when people put you down or belittle you in what God has called you to do, as if they themselves are called to authenticate the directives of the Holy Spirit. How many times have I wanted to dance circles of spiritual truth around some arrogant know-it-all preachers who were clearly snubbing their noses at me. It was the superior look of theological snobbery that I just could not stomach, yet it would require stooping just as low to respond.

I remember all too well the cost of such arrogance. Now don't get me wrong, it hurt tremendously not to say something, or at least put on a show of how much more well versed I was in spiritual knowledge, yet the Holy Spirit was near to my heart guarding my thoughts and convicting my conscience against any attempt by me that would bring a reproach to the ministry of Christ. I found the benefit of studying the Apostle's life in the scriptures as a form of discipline to my own soul. Examining how he handled both the people and the word. He confronted the darkened minds in his day with revelation and truth. Through the Holy Spirit, Paul becomes a guard in the gateway of truth as he exposes the treachery of Satan, who manipulates the greed and selfish ambition of the false teachers and weak Christians.

He confronts their shameful hypocrisy of the need for man's commendation with the reality that a changed life is already the greatest commendation one can receive. All these years I have felt like I was in the academic halls of heaven, receiving a proper education through the life of this Apostle. Throughout my time under the discipline of the Holy Spirit, I have had the good fortune of examining people in Paul's day and through my own encounters. My conclusion remains that there is no Condemnation in Christ!

Three things stand out as primary themes in my spiritual education, which I like to call, "an earthly walk with a heavenly God":

1.   The Dysfunction of Darkness
2.   The Purity of the Good News
3.   Mantle of Grace.

The Dysfunction of Darkness

When darkness operates in the life of the believer it creates spiritual dysfunction. It is the counterclockwise movement to the move of the Holy Spirit. You can be in this place and things can still feel right. You will even hear things in the spirit realm that you attribute to the Holy Spirit, but it is not from Him. This is the work of darkness appearing as light.

Without the help of the Spirit of God you will not even be aware of this deception until it is exposed and revealed as deception. Dysfunction is when a relationship operates or functions outside of the boundaries that make it healthy, whole and productive. At least that is what it means to me. The Holy Spirit has taken up residence in our lives and calls our body His home. He sets a careful watch over us, both guarding and alerting us to encounters with darkness that will result in the temptation to sin. He makes us aware of the hidden works of darkness within the soul aiding us in working out the salvation of our souls through the word of God. The thing He does not do is control our decision to heed to His counsel or His warnings, leaving us with the right to choose to yield or surrender in any direction we choose.

The hardest thing for me to come to grips with was my continued desire for a relationship with darkness even in my early walk with Christ. This inward desire was the gateway Satan exploited to bring about my destruction, that coupled with the pride that I allow to remain as a stronghold in my life. The times I flirted with temptation I needed that cloak of darkness to give me the comfort of pretending to be a victim. I felt better when I could excuse my rebellious behaviors as ignorance. I did not know what I was about to do, I did not plan it, I was an unwilling suspect. I did not see it coming, but I came to realize that was not the truth. The real truth was this was me taking comfort in the cloak of darkness. The term darkness can be a metaphor for many things. It can represent the absence of light, love and righteous goodness. It is in effect the absence of God. It can also mean the absence of truth and knowledge, an inability to find and walk in the paths of true righteousness. The bible uses the term darkness as a symbol of all of these things.

Despite how we choose to define or explain darkness one thing remains true, Satan uses this present darkness to ensnare and defeat mankind in the earth. Darkness is a device, we can use it or be used by it. It is a stronghold and a prison used to capture the souls of men. Man is incapable of producing light in and of himself, the bearer of all true light is Christ. We must commit to walking fully in obedience to Christ for His light to manifest fully in us
.

He is the light that entered into the world and our lamp. The Prophet Samuel said it this way, 2 Sam. 22:29- For you are my lamp; O LORD, And the LORD illumines my darkness. The ignorance of this spiritual truth has been the downfall of man, even after experiencing the salvation of God through Christ. Man, will fall prey to the devices of Satan and attempt to produce righteousness out of his own understanding. This is the inner working nature of self-righteousness.

Romans 1:21 states, For even though they knew God, they did not honor him as God or give thanks, but became futile in their speculations, and their foolish heart was darkened.

The implication is that knowing God without giving him honor, which produces thanksgiving can cause man to become fruitless or useless. In this state we are abandoned to empty assumptions, our hearts fill with foolishness and become dark. Unilluminated by his truth, dishonor leads us into great ignorance or darkness.

Matthew 6:22-23 explains it another way; "Your eyes are windows into your body. If you open your eyes wide in wonder and belief, your body fills up with light. If you live squinty-eyed in greed and distrust, your body is a dank cellar. If you pull the blinds on your windows, what a dark life you will have! (MSG)

This passage sheds light as to how the enemy of our souls takes advantage of our unbelief. If we view the world through greed and distrust we are blinded by our distorted opinion of life and what a great darkness that creates. We will live self- centered, paranoid lives, cut off from the realities that lie in trusting a loving God with our whole hearts. The greed will cause us to see everyone as we see ourselves, out to get some gain or advantage over us or other unsuspecting victims. Greed is the empty abyss that feeds off the lust in men's souls, unsatisfied and full of sorrow we drown in its ever- tightening grip, greed and distrust devour us in darkness.

Don't become partners with those who reject God. How can you make a partnership out of right and wrong? That's not partnership; that's war. Is light best friends with dark? Does Christ go strolling with the Devil? Do trust and mistrust hold hands? Who would think of setting up pagan idols in God's holy Temple? But that is exactly what we are, each of us a temple in whom God lives. God himself put it this way: "I'll live in them, move into them; I'll be their God and they'll be my people. So, leave the corruption and compromise; leave it for good," says God. "Don't link up with those who will pollute you". I want you all for myself. I'll be a Father to you; you'll be sons and daughters to me."-2 Corinthians 6:14-18

Paul vividly brings to light to the absurdity of compromise; in this passage he challenges the thought process of those around him who have been deceived into thinking there can be any co-existence between light and darkness. His approach of using a series of questions does not command that one stop doing these things, but that they consider how truly impossible the task is. Since a rational man will not willingly continue in such absurdity, he wills himself to stop. Two opposing kingdoms do not make a partnership, but a war, and anytime light is present darkness is dispelled.

Our struggle is to realize that God has chosen us to become his temple, thereby replacing all earthly temples with living temples. Ignorance of this spiritual truth can create quite the opportunity for Satan and his devices. In the latter part of the passage God himself reveals both his desire and his command for us to leave it all, the corruption, the compromise, mental and emotional idols. Nothing of the former life can remain, no partnership with the kingdom we have escaped through His grace and no relationship with those who would pollute us.

Our Lord did not leave us helpless in this endeavor to exercise power over our enemy. He gave us the Holy Spirit, who convicts us and the world of sin.

Conviction is drastically different from condemnation. Conviction has no part in punishment, rejection or accusation. Consider the prodigal son, I believe in some sense his lifestyle ultimately convicted him. Remembering his father's love and great compassion, he experienced sorrow over his current state, and the shipwreck he had made of his life. He knew he would be better off even as one of his father's servants. This sorrow led him to repentance and he returned to be completely restored by his father's love for him. Conviction puts our heart on notice to the truth of our heavenly father's great love for us. In Christ he has clothed us in the robes of righteousness, not the defiled tattered garment of sin and shame. In Christ we have the purest garment of his holiness, not the filthy garment of corruption. This convicting power of the Holy Spirit brings our focus back to the truth of his endless love and causes us to long to be restored to our rightful position. Knowing how great are the riches we possess in Christ, who in one's right mind would willingly choose to live beneath such divine privilege.

We must remember that every invitation to resist the reality of God's goodness is turned into an opportunity for Satan to ensnare us in darkness. This decision to yield to the invitation of temptation results in ignorance that truly blinds the mind, trapping us in a prison of darkness that can only be escaped when we repent and humbly receive God's over our own perceived reality.

As Christians this darkness can be in our understanding, when our counsel is darkened or veiled, as Paul revealed to the Corinthians who were veiled in their understanding of the new covenant.

"The Government of Death, its constitution chiseled on stone tablets, had a dazzling inaugural. Moses' face as he delivered the tablets was so bright that day (even though it would fade soon enough) that the people of Israel could no more look right at him than stare into the sun. How much more dazzling, then, the Government of Living Spirit? - 2 Corinthians 2:7-18;

If the Government of Condemnation was impressive, how about this Government of Affirmation? Bright as that old government was, it would look downright dull alongside this new one. If that makeshift arrangement impressed us, how much more this brightly shining government installed for eternity?

With that kind of hope to excite us, nothing holds us back. Unlike Moses, we have nothing to hide. Everything is out in the open with us. He wore a veil so the children of Israel wouldn't notice that the glory was fading away—and they didn't notice. They didn't notice it then and they don't notice it now, don't notice that there's nothing left behind that veil. Even today when the proclamations of that old, bankrupt government are read out, they can't see through it. Only Christ can get rid of the veil so they can see for themselves that there's nothing there. Whenever, though, they turn to face God as Moses did, God removes the veil and there they are—face-to-face!

They suddenly recognize that God is a living, personal presence, not a piece of chiseled stone. And when God is personally present, a living Spirit, that old, constricting legislation is recognized as obsolete. We're free of it! All of us! Nothing between us and God, our faces shining with the brightness of his face. And so we are transfigured much like the Messiah, our lives gradually becoming brighter and more beautiful as God enters our lives and we become like him".

The Christian of Paul's day, like many today had trouble believing the simplicity of the gospel and the liberty it produced in the life of the believer. In ignorance, they clung to the old covenant given under Moses, even though the new covenant in Christ was more excellent. They fell prey to the pride and ambition of their own teachings in the face of God's truth. This truth was that no law and no human effort could save man from plunging into the depths of a burning hell. This truth was that the soul is utterly lost without the redeeming blood of God's own sacred Lamb. The truth of the law was that it only came to reveal sin not to remove it. It exposed the harsh reality of how deep and wide our separation from God was as a result of disobedience. Our sin against God had produced the veil that would continue to separate us until the penalty had been satisfied, not just by blood, but by death.

This veil would not be removed from the natural temple until Christ had met the requirement the law demanded, (the wages of sin is death) once satisfied the veil in the temple was rent from top to bottom. It granted us the restoration of direct and intimate access to God which had been promised. The veil over man's heart can only be removed when Jesus, and Jesus alone is received on the merits of the cross and its finished work as the only means of obtaining salvation. This selfless act of grace is so incredible that nothing can be added to it or taken away from it, without disqualifying ourselves in receiving it. The veil of pride, self- righteousness and vain glory is a tool in the hands of our enemy. Paul speaks of this veil as a tool, concealing and hiding the truth that is only to be revealed in Christ. Paul exposes how the enemy of our souls uses our ignorance of the terms of our new covenant in Christ against us. He draws stark contrast between the two covenants as he did in Romans with light and darkness.

The differences are striking as we will examine. The most obvious difference is that the former covenant and law was outward in its manifestation. It was written on tablets of stone contained in a physical ark made of wood, stored in a temple made of human hands though the plans for the construction of the temple came directly from God. The spiritual truth that all of this pointed directly to Christ and who He was to the world as a Savior is usually lost in our observation of the splendor of this former design.

Jesus Christ brought God down to us, not in wrath, but in mercy, not in punishment but in forgiveness. He did not come in judgement, but He came in forgiveness, offering us a pardon through His blood. Where the previous law demanded a continuous payment of repeated atonement, the temporary atonement of animal blood was insufficient to remove guilt and only delayed payment for another day. The atonement Jesus offered in ratifying the new covenant is eternal and has completely satisfied God's demand for just payment in full. As believers who demonstrate sincere faith in the finished work of Christ we are justified in our faith as Abraham was also counted righteous in His faith in God. Now the new covenant is manifested inwardly, the law of God is written on the table of the human heart. Not a stony heart but a tender heart, one that is open and responsive to the voice of his Spirit, A heart that is open and willing to be implanted with His word and imprinted with his presence.

The human heart through faith in Jesus Christ becomes the ark of the new covenant. The life of the believer becomes the new temple.

So profound is the statement "Know you not that you are the temple of the Holy Spirit". Yet, with our old covenant mentality we do more to beautify and dress the temples made by hands (big elaborate buildings with ornate furnishings) rather than our own born-again temples made by His Spirit. We constantly neglect the new temple – the human body and the precious cargo it carries, while being obsessed with buildings made of human hands, as we strain to build them to perfection in hopes that God will meet us when we go there.

The false teachers of Paul's day magnified the Law of Moses and its obsession with sin and wrath neglecting to teach the people that the Law focused on death and a God who was above us. The good news of the Gospel revealed Emmanuel- God with us and for us. Jesus manifested to the world, he is the only way back to God our Father.

6-7 Jesus said, "I am the Road, also the Truth, also the Life. No one gets to the Father apart from me. If you really knew me, you would know my Father as well. From now on, you do know him. You've even seen him!"- John 14:6-7 (MSG);

The new covenant satisfied in the blood of Jesus what the old covenant could only reveal. Sin and its penalty of death quenched forever and God brought near to man in the cross, making restoration possible for all who would ever dare to believe. The bible records that at the death of Christ the veil in the temple area called the holy of holies, which contained the Ark of the Covenant was torn from top to bottom. The temple itself was later destroyed around A.D. 70, but the veil on some men's hearts and mind remains to this day.   One of the biggest snares for believers today is continuing to live under the code of the law. Making them a transgressor to the whole law and giving place to the enemy through condemnation as I myself once did.

The Purity of the Good News

The bible uses words and phrases to describe the word of God that leave us with pictures painted on our imagination that can't be misunderstood, such as pure milk, newborn babes desire the sincere milk. These words reveal the simplicity of the spiritual diet and the genuine state of helpless dependency of the new believer on those responsible for feeding them. Let's examine some different translations of the same passage of scripture to further emphasize this point

1 Peter 2:2:

Like newborn babies, crave pure spiritual milk, so that by it you may grow up in your salvation, - 1 Peter 2:2 (NIV)

Like newborn infants, long for the pure spiritual milk, that by it you may grow up into salvation ESV

As newborn babes, desire the sincere milk of the word, that ye may grow thereby: KJV

Babies have no control over what a guardian will try to feed them, but they have a naturally instinctive desire for milk. The sincerest form of milk comes from the breast of a healthy nursing mother. We are directed to desire or crave spiritual milk. We do not crave any type of milk, but pure or sincere milk. The word pure denotes something without additives or contaminates, a substance that is not harsh or in any way harmful. The word sincere speaks of the Word of God as being without pretense or deceit, genuine. From a human perspective it would be cruel to give a newborn unhealthy, contaminated, or spoiled milk, neither would you feed a newborn hamburger or chicken. A good guardian would recognize the fragile nature of the baby's digestive system, while a healthy baby would crave or desire this wholesome beverage which is demonstrated by the natural sucking instinct when a newborn is hungry. This picture presents the argument that both the giver and the receiver have a role to play, also that the word of God, in and of itself is Holy, pure undefiled without guile.

This is how the commentator Matthew Henry spoke of guile:

"Guile, or deceit in words. So, it comprehends flattery, falsehood, and delusion, which is a crafty imposing upon another's ignorance or weakness, to his damage." Matthew Henry further expounds on the above verse pertaining to this spiritual milk;

"This milk of the word must be sincere, not adulterated by the mixtures of men, who often corrupt the word of God". - (2 Corinthians. 2:17)

"The manner in which they are to desire this sincere milk of the word is stated thus: As newborn babes. He puts them in mind of their regeneration. A new life requires suitable food. They, being newly born, must desire the milk of the word. Infants desire common milk, and their desires towards it are fervent and frequent, arising from an impatient sense of hunger, and accompanied with the best endeavors of which the infant is capable. Such must Christians' desires be for the word of God: and that for this end, that they may grow thereby, that we may improve in grace and the knowledge of our Lord and Saviour, 2 Peter. 3:1   Learn, 1. Strong desires and affections to the word of God are a sure evidence of a person's being born again. If they be such desires as the babe has for the milk, they prove that the person is newborn. They are the lowest evidence, but yet they are certain. 2. Growth and improvement in wisdom and grace are the design and desire of every Christian; all spiritual means are for edification and improvement. The word of God, rightly used, does not leave a man as it finds him, but improves and makes him better."

Many of the false teachers of Paul's day failed to rightly use the word of God often leaving the hearer confused, or deceived; as Paul would point out in his letters, they imposed their craftiness in mishandling the word of God as a means of taking advantage of the ignorance of their audience. The same treacherous behavior exists among the false teachers of our present day.

We can thus conclude that if the Word is perverted or contaminated, it is due to the one delivering it to this newborn. Either by adding something harmful or removing something substantive to the growth of a new born believer. There is also a requirement placed on the one coming to God's kingdom. The other scenario is when the new born believer does not want to enter the kingdom as a child.

Matthew 18:3 "Truly I tell you," He said, "unless you change and become like little children, you will never enter the kingdom of heaven. (NIV)

This passage speaks to the posture of the one desiring this newfound relationship with God. It is the quality and the character of becoming lowly as our Savior came to us that pleases God. It reflects the beauty of undertaking a spirit of submission as we yield ourselves to God's authority and his covering. At the finest of times, in training children the honorable child did not exalt himself in pride against an elder brother, nor did children relish in distasteful, pretentious, or pious behaviors. Children were taught to show honor with reverence, humility, and love. In addition, children were trusting of a loving parent. It is hard to shake the confidence of a child who is the recipient of a caring parent's full love.

The responsibility for preserving the integrity of presenting the Gospel with simplicity is to be shared by all who love Christ. Both the presenter and the listener must bear in this duty. Paul so eloquently brought out this point in his letter to the Thessalonians

1 Thessalonians 2;1;
" So, friends, it's obvious that our visit to you was no waste of time. We had just been given rough treatment in Philippi, as you know, but that didn't slow us down. We were sure of ourselves in God, and went right ahead and said our piece, presenting God's Message to you, defiant of the opposition.

God tested us thoroughly to make sure we were qualified to be trusted with this Message. Be assured that when we speak to you we're not after crowd approval—only God approval. Since we've been put through that battery of tests, you're guaranteed that both we and the Message are free of error, mixed motives, or hidden agendas. We never used words to butter you up. No one knows that better than you. And God knows we never used words as a smoke screen to take advantage of you.

Even though we had some standing as Christ's apostles, we never threw our weight around or tried to come across as important, with you or anyone else. We weren't aloof with you. We took you just as you were. We were never patronizing, never condescending, but we cared for you the way a mother cares for her children. We loved you dearly". - (Msg)

Paul shares that the heart of a leader is not content to just pass on the message, we wanted to give you our hearts. He says, and we did. He speaks of his time with them as a worthy investment, revealing the selfless nature of his commitment to the Lord and his flock. We see from the passage that there is a certain amount of testing or proving we must go through in order to be found trustworthy. It is not just the ability to carry the Good News, but we must carry it with Godly character and spiritual integrity, without false motives or hidden agendas. It is equally important to note that we all struggle with the same temptations for vain glory, selfish ambition and various prides in and of life, and we overcome them through the things that we suffer. This process prepares us in the Holy Spirit to be willing to walk in the type of humility and surrender that frees us of errors, mixed motives and hidden agendas.

Paul also understood the major role suffering plays in the development of Godly character and mature spiritual growth. Through his own suffering godly character was developed and it would prepare him to later reign with Christ. Paul gives insight into how his maturity coupled with humility afforded him and his followers to make the most of the advantages they had through God's grace. He did not Lord over them or throw his weight around as one better or above them. He did not flaunt his authority, but submitted both his grace and his strength in the service of the Lord for their benefit. This benefit was their spiritual growth and maturity in Christ even when their immaturity did not always allow them to appreciate such a sacrifice, Paul remained confident that the pure deposit of Gods undefiled word given in love would bear appropriate fruit in them over time. Paul was trustworthy in his commitment to feed and care for the Lord's dear children as he often called them and so we must endeavor to do the same in the grace of God. Paul ends his point by stating that "We cared for you the way a mother cares for her children".

This brings us back to our point of how a mother would feed a newborn. If the new baby did not have a desire for milk, the good sound mother would question the health of the child as there must surely be a problem for a newborn to have no appetite. This is as much a spiritual truth to, every new convert to Christ should display evidence of this hunger and appetite for the sincere milk of the Word of God. Without a hunger met with an appropriate diet, there would be no growth. At its worst, it would result in loss of life, or severe retardation, or at least it would result in slow or perverted development.

We all can conclude that if young children are fed the wrong things or too much of the same things, such as sweets they will suffer in their developmental years. Teeth will rot from too much sugar, vitamin deficiencies will hinder the immune system and so much more, in the same way we can't afford to only preach what people want to hear; eliminating scriptures that challenge us or our lifestyle choices.

We can't preach just from the old testament or only about the Prophets, we must give a full gospel as the Holy Spirit leads and instructs us; without fear or making a watered-down attempt to butter up the heart of the listener, give them the full counsel of God. A novice or a peddler of the Word, one who merchandizes the Gospel to their own gains, will not submit to such instruction. Many will only preach what is profitable. The Novice lacks the maturity and the discipline, this individual is a beginner. Though a novice may be smart and catch hold to the truths of God's word quickly, they lack skill in so many other areas and have not been tried in the heart, where Godly character is formed. They are true spiritual rookies or greenhorns as some would say.
I was such a novice in the beginning and it brought me to the end of myself, but the fruit of my submission has brought me to the Apostles Mantle, which I will share with just one passage of scripture.

Ephesians 4:11-15 Amplified Bible (AMP)
11 And [His gifts to the church were varied and] He Himself appointed some as apostles [special messengers, representatives], some as prophets [who speak a new message from God to the people], some as evangelists [who spread the good news of salvation], and some as pastors and teachers [to shepherd and guide and instruct], 12 [and He did this] to fully equip and perfect the saints (God's people) for works of service, to build up the body of Christ [the church]; 13 until we all reach oneness in the faith and in the knowledge of the Son of God, [growing spiritually] to become a mature believer, reaching

to the measure of the fullness of Christ [manifesting His spiritual completeness and exercising our spiritual gifts in unity]. 14 So that we are no longer children [spiritually immature], tossed back and forth [like ships on a stormy sea] and carried about by every wind of [shifting] doctrine, by the cunning and trickery of [unscrupulous] men, by the deceitful scheming of people ready to do anything [for personal profit]. 15 But speaking the truth in love [in all things—both our speech and our lives expressing His truth], let us grow up in all things into Him [following His example] who is the Head—Christ.

I came into the ministry at a time when this was not taught or even fully accepted as relevant. I had good leaders but they were not apostolically informed. Today I could say had I been under a more fully informed covering things may have been very different for me. Then again, I would not be sharing this with you today. By God's grace I am who I am because of what I've been through and in-spite of it. I pray that my words have encouraged and inspired you.

Remember, Beware of wolves – they are among us!

CPSIA information can be obtained
at www.ICGtesting.com
Printed in the USA
LVHW030923240222
711901LV00003B/300